YUMMY!

Eating Through a Day

Poems selected by Lee Bennett Hopkins

Illustrated by Renée Flower

SIMON & SCHUSTER BOOKS FOR YOUNG READERS

ARTIST'S NOTE

My illustrations begin as pencil sketches on tracing paper. I place the type under the tracing paper and draw around it so it becomes part of the illustration. When I'm happy with the sketch, I transfer it to a smooth artist's drawing paper. The illustrations are then painted with watercolor and gouache and embellished with scratches for texture and pattern. Some larger areas are painted with a sponge to create either a speckled surface, or a smooth velvetlike effect. I use color pencils for details and black pastel for outlines and shadows. I work on all of the paintings at once, moving from one to the other until they feel like a family.

—RENÉE FLOWER

To Rebecca Davis and John Tarangelo—for yummy-years — L. B. H.

In memory of Frank, my little Meezer friend — R. F.

SIMON & SCHUSTER BOOKS FOR YOUNG READERS
An imprint of Simon & Schuster Children's Publishing Division, 1230 Avenue of the Americas, New York, New York 10020. Text copyright © 2000 by Lee Bennett Hopkins. Illustrations copyright © 2000 by Renée Flower. All rights reserved including the right of reproduction in whole or in part in any form. SIMON & SCHUSTER BOOKS FOR YOUNG READERS is a trademark of Simon & Schuster. Book design by Lily Malcom. The text for this book is set in Triplex. Printed in Hong Kong. 10 9 8 7 6 5 4 3 2 1 Page 32 constitutes an extension of this copyright page. Library of Congress Cataloging-in-Publication Data. Yummy! : eating through a day / poems selected by Lee Bennett Hopkins ; illustrated by Renée Flower.   p.   cm. Summary: A collection of poems about all different kinds of foods—from cereal and oranges to pasta, potato chips, and peas. ISBN 0-689-81755-X   1. Food—Juvenile poetry. 2. Children's poetry, American. [1. Food—Poetry. 2.Poetry—Collections.] I. Hopkins, Lee Bennett. II. Flower, Renée, ill. PS595.F65Y86 2000. 811.008'0355—dc21 98-38507. CIP AC

first edition

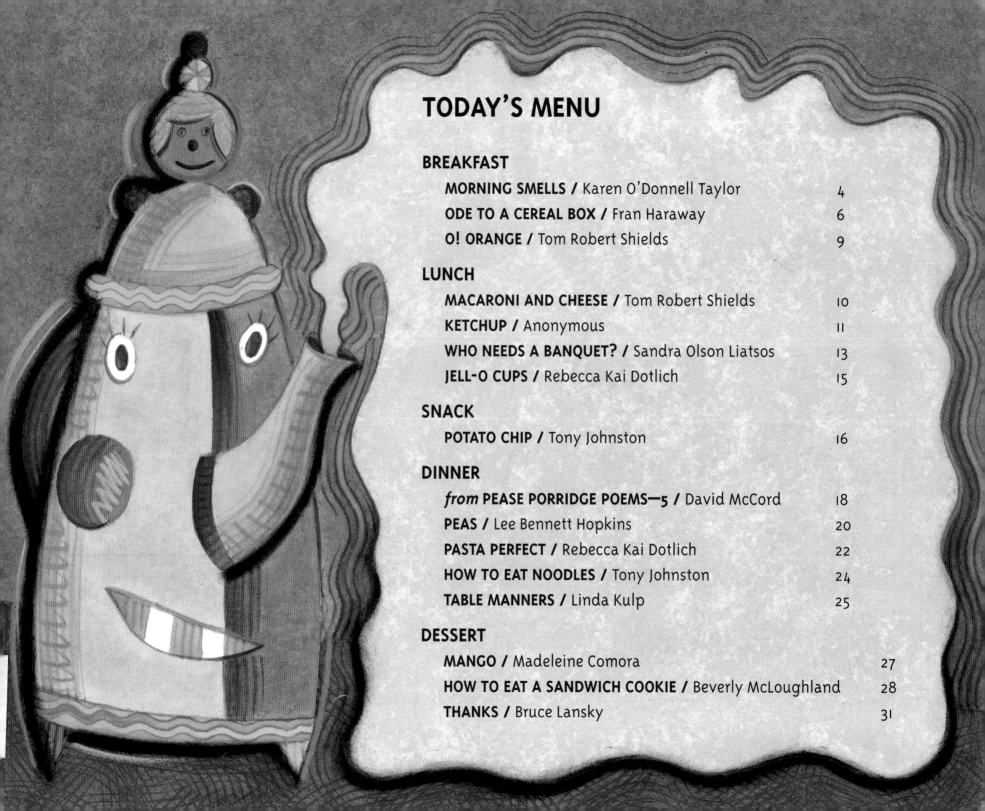

TODAY'S MENU

Morning Smells

Karen O'Donnell Taylor

Morning smells like bacon.
It laces through the air,
drifting 'round the kitchen
winding up the stair.

It slips beneath my doorway
creeps up past my chin,
wakes me oh, so gently
as I breathe the sweetness in.

Cinnamon buns are baking,
mingling with the smell
of sharp, strong coffee
and frying eggs as well.

Sweet smells reach my room. . . .
No need for Mom to knock.
When morning smells delicious,
I wake without a clock.

Ode to a Cereal Box

Fran Haraway

I strike,
I shred,
I smash,
I stab,

I rip,
I rend,
I grip,
I grab,

I jiggle,
      jostle,
      jolt,
      and jab

but—

cannot
budge
the

"Lift this tab."

8

O! Orange

Tom Robert Shields

Perfect morning roundness
Color from the sun
Pebbly sort of cover
Over pure white silky skin.

Divided equal sections
Seeds, liquid, pulp, too.

O! Orange of tropic pleasure
I squeeze sweet juice from you.

Macaroni and Cheese

Tom Robert Shields

If you take
All the macaroni and cheese
I eat
Place it noodle to noodle
With all that cheesy goo
It would stretch from here
To Aunt Bea's house.

Better her than me.
I'm sick of macaroni and cheese.

Ketchup

Anonymous

When you tip
and tip
the ketchup bottle—

A little will come
and then
a lot'll.

11

Who Needs a Banquet?

Sandra Olson Liatsos

Who needs a banquet
fit for kings?
Who needs a heap
of jeweled rings?
Who needs a million
dollar jet
or a diamond collar
for a pet?
When bubbly pizza
from the oven
makes me grab
my fork and knife,
I need no more—
except a plate,
to lead a happy
pizza life.

Jell-O Cups

Rebecca Kai Dotlich

Cups of Jell-O
blue
and yellow,
 wiggle
waggle
  jiggle
jaggle.

Dancing squares
squirm
and shake,
  bright red *shiver*,
quiver,
  quake.

Rainbow cubes
on plates,
in cups
lemon,
  lime,

we *s l u r p* them up.

15

Potato Chip

Tony Johnston

When I slip one into my mouth
its crisp tongue tells me
salty secrets.

16

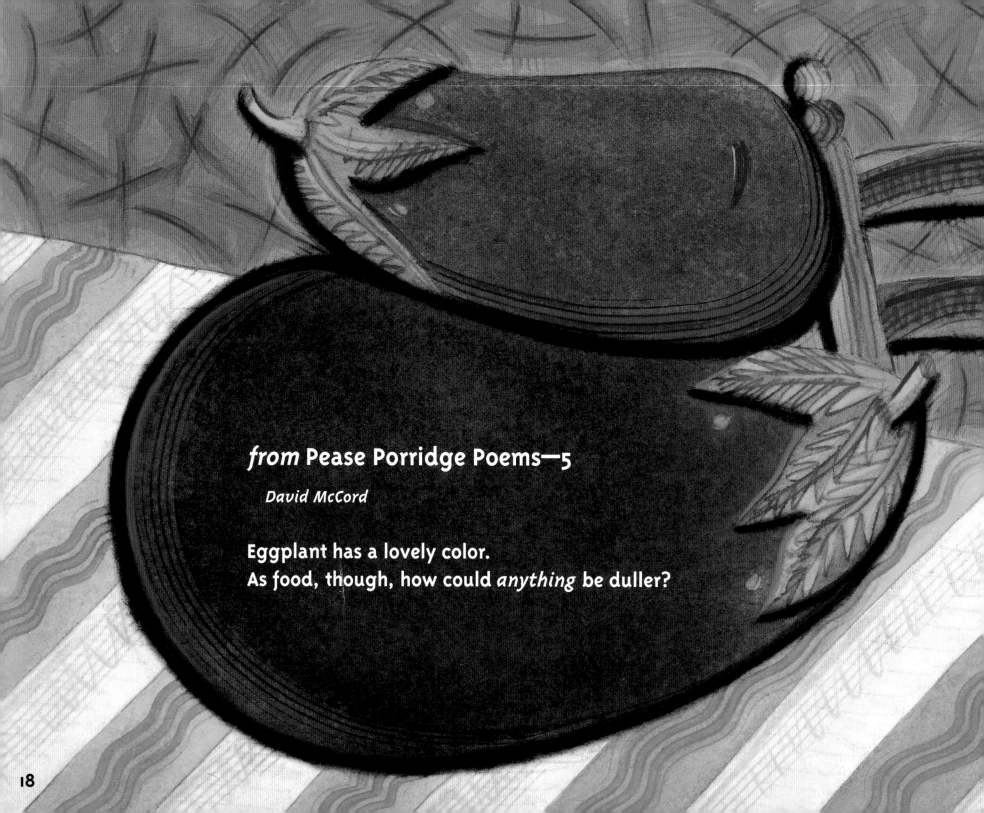

from Pease Porridge Poems—5

David McCord

Eggplant has a lovely color.
As food, though, how could *anything* be duller?

Peas

Lee Bennett Hopkins

Scattered
on the sidewalk
outside of Nellie's Deli
split peas
from a
shattered
plastic bag
flow.

A pea-green
fright!

Peas
that were
supposed to be
our pea-soup
supper
tonight!

Pasta Perfect

Rebecca Kai Dotlich

Ravioli.
Macaroni.
Vermicelli
in the pot.
Tortellini.
Cappellini
steamy hot.
Pasta in the shape of o's.
Pasta tied
in ruffled bows.
Pasta buttered
boiled
and tossed.
Pasta smothered
in a sauce.

Macaroni.
Ravioli.
Manicotti
strikes my mood.
Tortellini.
Thin linguini.
Pasta is
the *perfect* food!

23

How To Eat Noodles

Tony Johnston

Place the tip of one noodle
into your mouth
so it droops in a slippery
ribbon
down your chin.
Don't grin: Pout your lips out
in a prim little "ooh"
like a bird about to chirp.
Then—
slurp.

Table Manners

Linda Kulp

No burping
No slurping
No giggling
No wiggling
No hitting
No spitting
No jabbing
No grabbing
No groaning
No moaning
No kicking
No picking
or sticking
your food
on the floor.

Table manners
make eating a bore!

Mango

Madeleine Comora

Bathed in flames
of sunset red
and gold
it beams
in the bowl.
I cradle
the ripe globe,
peel away the skin,
perfume rises,
thick juice drips
on my chin.
The pulp,
sticky sweet,
cools
the summer heat
down to the oval stone,
slippery smooth
and white as the moon.

27

How To Eat a Sandwich Cookie

Beverly McLoughland

A rookie
Cookie eater
Eats a sandwich cookie
Fast—
1 bite, 2 bite—
End of cookie.

A pro
Makes a sandwich cookie
Last—
Knows the art
Of getting to the cookie's
Heart—
Slides the halves
Apart—
Ver-y
Ver-y
Slowly,
Bottom
Against top.
       Stops.

Turns the top side
Over . . .
             Yes!
One round and creamy
Sugar moon.

Of course
A pro *always* eats
The blank side
First—
And then,
With a silly grin,
And a thank you
Very much—

Eats the half
That holds
The soft vanilla
Moon.

Thanks

Bruce Lansky

Thanks for the story
and thanks for the drink
you brought all the way
from the bathroom sink.
Thanks for the backrub;
I've just one more wish:
a chocolate sundae
with nuts in a dish!

31

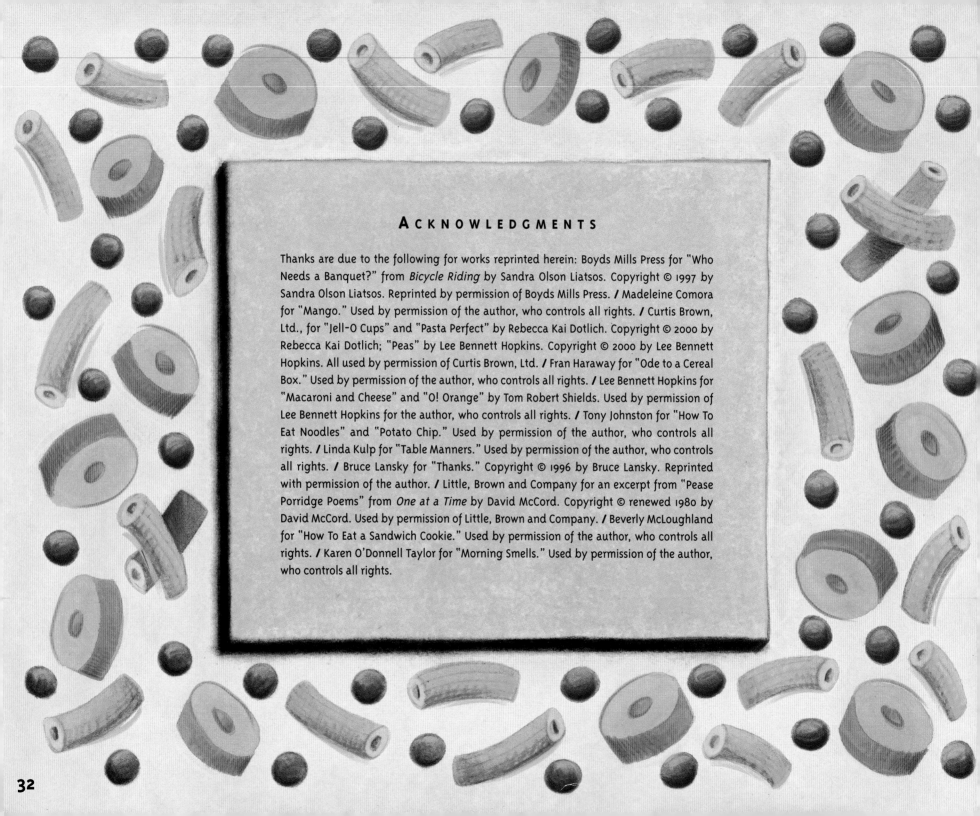

ACKNOWLEDGMENTS

Thanks are due to the following for works reprinted herein: Boyds Mills Press for "Who Needs a Banquet?" from *Bicycle Riding* by Sandra Olson Liatsos. Copyright © 1997 by Sandra Olson Liatsos. Reprinted by permission of Boyds Mills Press. / Madeleine Comora for "Mango." Used by permission of the author, who controls all rights. / Curtis Brown, Ltd., for "Jell-O Cups" and "Pasta Perfect" by Rebecca Kai Dotlich. Copyright © 2000 by Rebecca Kai Dotlich; "Peas" by Lee Bennett Hopkins. Copyright © 2000 by Lee Bennett Hopkins. All used by permission of Curtis Brown, Ltd. / Fran Haraway for "Ode to a Cereal Box." Used by permission of the author, who controls all rights. / Lee Bennett Hopkins for "Macaroni and Cheese" and "O! Orange" by Tom Robert Shields. Used by permission of Lee Bennett Hopkins for the author, who controls all rights. / Tony Johnston for "How To Eat Noodles" and "Potato Chip." Used by permission of the author, who controls all rights. / Linda Kulp for "Table Manners." Used by permission of the author, who controls all rights. / Bruce Lansky for "Thanks." Copyright © 1996 by Bruce Lansky. Reprinted with permission of the author. / Little, Brown and Company for an excerpt from "Pease Porridge Poems" from *One at a Time* by David McCord. Copyright © renewed 1980 by David McCord. Used by permission of Little, Brown and Company. / Beverly McLoughland for "How To Eat a Sandwich Cookie." Used by permission of the author, who controls all rights. / Karen O'Donnell Taylor for "Morning Smells." Used by permission of the author, who controls all rights.